KU-635-562

Trump and Me

MARK SINGER

WITH A FOREWORD BY
DAVID REMNICK

PENGUIN BOOKS

PENGUIN BOOKS

UK | USA | Canada | Ireland | Australia
India | New Zealand | South Africa

Penguin Books is part of the Penguin Random House group of companies
whose addresses can be found at global.penguinrandomhouse.com.

First published in the United States of America by Tim Duggan Books,
an imprint of the Crown Publishing Group, a division of
Penguin Random House LLC 2016
First published in Great Britain by Allen Lane 2016
Published in Penguin Books 2016

010

Set in 11/16 pt Epic Book
Printed in Great Britain by Clays Ltd, St Ives plc

A CIP catalogue record for this book is available from the British Library

ISBN: 978-0-141-98489-6

www.greenpenguin.co.uk

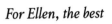

For Ellen, the best

CONTENTS

FOREWORD

For decades, the problem posed by Donald Trump to writers, whether it was a daily tabloid reporter or a more high-minded scribe for what used to be known as "the qualities," was that he was beyond parody. A man of rampaging ego, sufficient funds, and a neediness greater than that of an infant, Trump bestrode New York City, littering the press with one fantastical quotation after another. He was the reliable La Rochefoucauld of our city. But instead of "Hypocrisy is a tribute that vice pays to virtue," we got "I have so many fabulous friends who happen to be gay, but I am a traditionalist."

In the pages of the satirical magazine *Spy* or in the *New York Post,* Trump was, in the '80s and '90s and later, a constant. He would not have wanted it any other way. He was a real-estate marketer and he sold himself wherever he could: there he was in the corner for a World Wide Wrestling match, or humiliating wannabe Trumps on *The Apprentice,* or demeaning half the human race on *The Howard Stern Show.* This was a gentleman who went on the radio to say of his former wife, "Nice tits, no brains." His vulgarity was unstoppable and without limit. He didn't much care if he came off as a little crude. He knew you couldn't resist listening. "You know," he said, "it doesn't really matter what they write as long as you've got a young and beautiful piece of ass."

Not only was Trump beyond insult or parody, he seemed a distinctly local product, like the smell of a Times Square subway platform in mid-August. In 1960, A. J. Liebling, *The New Yorker*'s polymathic reporter of midcentury, set out for Louisiana to write about Governor Earl Long, Huey's more erratic brother, with a similar conviction that his subject was not for export. "Southern political personalities, like sweet corn, travel badly," he wrote. "By the time they reach New York, they are like Golden Bantam that has been trucked up from Texas—stale and unprofitable." This was the problem with Trump in reverse.

I suspect that these factors were at the root of my friend and colleague Mark Singer's initial reluctance to write about Donald Trump when, in 1996, his editor, Tina Brown, more or less commanded him to do so. I can vouch for the genuineness of Mark's initial reluctance. I have seen him when he is captivated by a subject—a bank collapse in his home state of Oklahoma, the wonders of the magician and scholar Ricky Jay—but he took a long time to warm to this one. But I am glad he felt the lash of editorial compulsion and moved ahead, if grudgingly, because, as it turned out, he provided us with the best, most insightful, and funniest portrait of Trump. Just as Liebling managed to make an export literary product out of half-mad Earl Long, so, too, did Singer find a way to write with freshness and wit about Trump. His profile is a classic of the form.

We just did not know that it would be of such value at this late date, for, as I write, Donald Trump is no longer interested merely in accruing another gold-plated tower in Manhattan; he intends to take occupancy of the White House. He intends to command the nation's armed forces and be in possession of its nuclear codes.

I'll never be sure, but I think I was in the room when Trump might have made his fateful determination to run for President. He had verbally and publically teased us with the idea for many years, but we always figured it was a publicity vehicle, like Trump Steaks. But I think at least some part of his decision to go forward was rooted in humiliation. At the 2011 White House Correspondents' Dinner, a springtime ritual of low moment, the press and the capital's politicians squeezed their egos into the biggest ballroom at the Hilton to preen, feed, and determine, yet again, who is funnier: the President of the United States or the hired-hand comedian invited to the dance.

That night President Obama, with the help of his speechwriters, decided the time was right to take off after Trump, who had been leading the effort to de-legitimize him by questioning his place of birth. Earlier in the week, the State of Hawaii had released Obama's "long-form" birth certificate, confirming, if anyone believed otherwise, that he had been born in a hospital in Honolulu. In his speech, Obama joked that he was now ready to go "a step further" and release his "birth video." What the crowd at the Hilton saw was a clip from *The Lion King*.

Obama knew that Trump was in the ballroom, seated at a table hosted by the *Washington Post* Company. The onslaught was prolonged.

"I know that he's taken some flack lately—no one is prouder to put this birth-certificate matter to rest than The Donald," Obama said, as many hundreds of eyes turned to Trump. "And that's because he can finally get back to focusing on the issues that matter, like: Did we fake the moon landing? What really happened in Roswell? And where are Biggie and Tupac?"

Trump's eyes narrowed. He clenched his jaw, pursed his lips. He was intensely displeased. Not for him the custom of smiling and taking it on the chin. This was easy to see. (I was just a couple of tables away.)

"All kidding aside, obviously, we all know about your credentials and breadth of experience," Obama said, thrusting the shiv deeper. "For example—no, seriously—just recently, in an episode of *Celebrity*

Apprentice, at the steakhouse the men's cooking team did not impress the judges from Omaha Steaks. And there was a lot of blame to go around. But you, Mr. Trump, recognized that the real problem was a lack of leadership. So ultimately you didn't blame Lil Jon or Meat Loaf. You fired Gary Busey. And these are the kinds of decisions that would keep me up at night. Well handled, sir!"

Seth Meyers, the comedian on duty that night, also came up with Trump material. His most memorable one-liner was: "Donald Trump has been saying he would run for President as a Republican. Which is surprising since I just assumed that he was running as a joke."

Again, I cannot be sure that this was the decisive night that resentment and jealousy turned to determined planning. Trump has denied it. Besides, no one paid much attention. The Trump moment at the dinner was eclipsed within hours when Obama announced that a team of Navy SEALs had killed Osama bin Laden.

This election season is surely the most preposterous and disheartening that we have experienced in decades. And Donald Trump's demagoguery, and his undeniable success in winning many more votes than anyone might have imagined, is the central reason. It is well worth going back to Mark Singer's profile to experience what it was to observe and think about the man when the stakes were so much lower and he was little more than my beloved city's semi-harmless buffoon.

—David Remnick

ONE ON ONE

It's the fall of 1996. I've been a staff writer at *The New Yorker* since 1974, I've worked for a number of editors, and at this point Tina Brown is the editor. Those proverbial tales of adversarial relationships between writers and editors?—I've managed to avoid all that. I like Tina. She and I have a clear working understanding. I've just spent four years writing a book that was supposed to have taken me a year and a half, during which I haven't been available to write many pieces for the magazine. So our understanding is that in Tina's office, in her desk, there is a special drawer. In that drawer is a jar. In that jar are my testicles.

One morning my phone rings—Tina: "Trump! Donald Trump! I've just had breakfast with him at the Plaza. You're going to write a profile of him. You're absolutely going to love him. He's totally full of shit, you'll love him! I've told him he'll love you. You're doing it!"

Which indicates that I am doing it.

I get to work. This takes several months. I go places with Trump. I try to understand his ways of doing business—the nuts and bolts, the smoke and mirrors. Early on, we reach our own working understanding: I tacitly accede to his assumption that I am his tool. It's Trump's world. I may watch and listen and occasionally ask questions. When permitted, I am a fly on a wall. Otherwise, as far as he's concerned, I don't really exist. This, by the way, I regard as optimal working conditions.

Unaccustomed though I am, I have to take Donald Trump seriously. Among other tasks, I must read many books with his name and photograph on the cover, ghostwritten books ostensibly composed by Trump. The overarching theme of this oeuvre would echo several years later, greatly amplified, in *The Apprentice*: *We both know that you're a complete putz, but you're at least allowed to fantasize about what my life is like.*

And that is in fact what I want to do. During our first encounter, in his office in Trump Tower, I grasp that, whoever or whatever I had previously imagined Trump to be, he is foremost a performance artist. Appearance is never not, at some level, artifice. My objective is to apprehend the person within the persona.

Many books and hundreds of articles have also been written about Trump, and I read those, too. There's no point in asking Trump questions he's answered in print already. Anyway, I can come up with a few new ones—say, does Donald Trump have an interior life? No one's ever asked him that, I bet.

One Saturday in the winter of 1997, he and I spend a morning and afternoon one on one, touring construction projects, in Manhattan (office building) and north of New York City, in Westchester County (golf courses). He drives and I sit in the death seat, taking notes. As we cruise up I-684, I ask about his early-morning routines.

What time do you wake up?

Five-thirty a.m.

What time do you arrive at your desk in the Trump Tower?

Seven or seven-thirty.

How do you spend your time before leaving for the office?

Reading the newspapers, etc.

"O.K.," I say. "You're basically alone. Your wife is still asleep"—he was then married, but not for much longer, to his second wife, Marla Maples—"you're in the bathroom shaving and you see yourself in the mirror. What are you thinking?"

From Trump, a look of incomprehension.

ME: "I mean, are you looking at yourself and thinking, 'Wow. I'm Donald Trump'?"

Trump remains puzzled.

ME: "O.K., I guess I'm asking, do you consider yourself ideal company?"

(At the time, I deemed Trump's reply unprintable. But that was then.)

TRUMP: "You really want to know what I consider ideal company?"

ME: "Yes."

TRUMP: "A total piece of ass."

On other occasions, for different reasons, I'm baffled by particular Trumpian locutions. He prefaces certain statements with "off-the-record but you can use it." This makes as much sense as his taxonomy of the real estate he sells: "Luxury, Super Luxury, and Super Super Luxury."

Spring arrives and the profile is almost finished. I have everything but an ending. I also have a deadline. Late on a Thursday night, I fax the story—ten thousand words, still no ending—to my editor. Ready for bed, I tap the clock radio on my night table, which is tuned to an all-news station. Top of the hour, the headline is: Donald Trump and Marla Maples are separating.

Inconveniently, I've seen none of this coming. Conveniently, my article has abruptly become timely. Trump agrees to meet with me in his office the following Monday, and my reward is an ending, an opening scene, and a crystalline certainty about his interior life. Given his domestic vicissitudes, is he happy? Regretful? Self-reflective? His demeanor gives away nothing. Previously, he's told me that in times of distress he confides in no one. Meanwhile, I've interviewed dozens of Trump associates and acquaintances, among them a securities analyst who observes, "Deep down, he wants to be Madonna."

All of which informs my conclusion that he does not have an interior life. The penultimate line: "He had aspired to and achieved the ultimate luxury, an existence unmolested by the rumbling of a soul."

Evidently, Trump does not appreciate what I've written. I don't hear from him directly, but he writes a spurned lover's complaint to Tina: "Don't ever ask me to do another story. You said, 'It will be great, you'll love it'—you lied!" The nerve.

Later that year, I gain a finer appreciation of his feelings toward me. He publishes *Trump: The Art of the Comeback,* ghostwritten by Kate Bohner, and devotes a few pages to Tina and me. He recounts that, years earlier, when Tina was the editor of *Vanity Fair,* she had assigned Marie Brenner ("an unattractive reporter") to write about him. For whatever reason, Trump omits what he once told me about how he'd exacted revenge—by pouring red wine down Marie's dress at a charity dinner.

There I am on page 181, in the chapter "The Press and Other Germs." (On the facing page is a photograph of Trump with Liberace, and the caption "Liberace was a great performer and a great man. We all miss him dearly." How true.)

Tina Brown was at it again, asking me to agree to a profile. She is a very persuasive woman. She told me, "You will love the piece, you'll absolutely love it!"

After listening a while, I agreed. I thought, how many editors call someone for breakfast in order to convince him to do a story that they could write without him anyway?

The next day I got a call from *The New Yorker*'s reporter, Mark Singer. When he came into the office, I immediately sensed that he was not much of anything, nondescript, with a faint wiseguy sneer and some kind of chip on his shoulder.

Singer reminded me a bit of Harry Hurt, a guy who wrote an inaccurate book about me. While Singer was slightly more physically attractive than Harry Hurt (which, by the way, wasn't difficult), Singer had *scar* written all over him.

Reading (and re-reading and re-reading!) this affirms, incontrovertibly, that my life has meaning. Other than the births of my children, nothing remotely this wonderful has ever happened. Should all else fall through or fade away, I will still have *Trump: The Art of the Comeback*.

Now it's 2005. I publish a book, *Character Studies*, that includes my reporting on Trump. In the Sunday *New York Times*, it's reviewed by Jeff MacGregor, who strikes me as a terrifically perceptive fellow, though he does have one quibble: "The only instance in which Singer throws and lands a sucker punch is in a 1997 profile of the pre-'Apprentice' Donald Trump, in which his tone becomes a little arch. That Trump is already a caricature of a caricature makes him too easy a target, with neither the foot speed nor the wit to defend himself."

Think again, MacGregor. Three weeks later, the *Times Book Review* features a letter from Trump about this review. A few days before the letter's publication, I learn that it's coming and decide to check my sales on Amazon. Alas, *Character Studies* is No. 45,638 on the best-seller list. No matter—Trump's letter is sublimely deranged:

To the Editor:

I can remember when Tina Brown was in charge of *The New Yorker* and a writer named Mark Singer interviewed me for a profile. He was depressed. I was thinking, O.K., expect the worst. Not only was Tina Brown dragging *The New Yorker* to a new low, this writer was drowning in his own misery, which could only put me in a skeptical mood regarding the outcome of their combined interest in me. Misery begets misery, and they were a perfect example of this credo.

Jeff MacGregor, the reviewer of *Character Studies*, a collection of Singer's *New Yorker* profiles, including the one about me, writes poorly. . . . Maybe he and Mark Singer belong together. Some people cast shadows, and other people choose to live in those shadows. To each his own. They are entitled to their choices.

Most writers want to be successful. Some writers even want to be good writers. I've read John Updike, I've read Orhan Pamuk, I've read Philip Roth. When Mark Singer enters their league, maybe I'll read one of his books. But it will be a long time—he was not born with great writing ability . . . Maybe he should . . . try to develop himself into a world-class writer, as futile as that may be, instead of having to write about remarkable people who are clearly outside of his realm.

I've been a best-selling author for close to 20 years. Whether you like it or not, facts are facts. The highly respected Joe Queenan mentioned in his article "Ghosts in the Machine" (March 20) that I had produced "a steady stream of classics" with "stylistic seamlessness" and that the "voice" of my books remained noticeably constant to the point of being an "astonishing achievement."*

This was high praise coming from an accomplished writer. From losers like Jeff MacGregor, whom I have never met, or Mark Singer, I do not do nearly as well. But I'll gladly take Joe Queenan over Singer and MacGregor any day of the week—it's a simple thing called talent!

I have no doubt that Singer's and MacGregor's books will do badly—they just don't have what it takes. Maybe someday they'll astonish us by writing something of consequence.

Donald Trump
New York

Within forty-eight hours, several fellow scribblers solicit advice on how to provoke Trump into attacking

* Lacking any aptitude for irony, Trump is blithely oblivious to Queenan's.

them, my book rockets to No. 385 on the Amazon list, and I hear my mother's voice reminding me to write a thank-you note. But I want to acknowledge my appreciation with more than a mere note. What should I send Trump? What does he like?

Money!

I decide to send him a thousand dollars.

Then it occurs to me that I don't have a thousand dollars. I come up with another figure.

Dear Donald,

Thank you so much for that wonderful letter to *The New York Times Book Review*. A number of friends have called or written to say that it's one of the funniest things they've read in a long time.

Though I'm sure that you, as an author, are aware that it's considered bad form to pay the people who review one's books, I nevertheless enclose a check for $37.82, a small token of my enormous gratitude. You're special to me.

Also, I enclose a couple of Band-Aids. Because you seem unable to stop picking at this particular scab, these should come in handy.

Cheerfully, Mark

I suspect that's not going to be the end of it and, indeed, ten days later I receive an envelope embossed with the Trump Organization logo and return address. Inside is my letter. Trump has returned it, inscribed in thick black all-caps: **"MARK, YOU ARE A TOTAL LOSER! AND YOUR BOOK (AND WRITINGS) SUCKS! BEST WISHES, DONALD. P.S. AND I HEAR IT IS SELLING BADLY."**

To his credit, he's correct about my anemic book sales. My Amazon ranking is already back down to 53,876.

Then one more thing happens. I get a letter from Citibank. I open it. Inside is my bank statement. My account, I see, is $37.82 lighter.

Trump has cashed the check.

MADONNA

One spring morning in 1997, Donald Trump, who under routine circumstances tolerates publicity no more grudgingly than an infant tolerates a few daily feedings, sat in his office on the twenty-sixth floor of Trump Tower, his mood rather subdued. As could be expected, given the fact that his three-and-a-half-year-old marriage to Marla Maples was ending, paparazzi were staking out the exits of Trump Tower, while all weekend helicopters had been hovering over Mar-a-Lago, his private club in Palm Beach. And what would come of it? "I think the thing I'm worst at is managing the press," he said. "The thing I'm best at is business and conceiving. The press portrays me as a wild flamethrower. In actuality, I think I'm much different from that. I think I'm totally inaccurately portrayed."

So, though he'd agreed to a conversation at this decisive moment, it called for wariness, the usual quota of prefatory "off-the-record"s and then some. He wore a navy-blue suit, white shirt, black-onyx-and-gold links, and a crimson print necktie. Every strand of his interesting hair—its gravity-defying ducktails and dry pompadour, its telltale absence of gray—was where he wanted it to be. He was working his way through his daily gallon of Diet Coke and trying out a few diversionary maneuvers. Yes, it was true, the end of a marriage was a sad thing. Meanwhile, was I aware of what a success he'd had with the Nation's Parade, the Veterans Day celebration he'd been very supportive of back in 1995? Well, here was a little something he wanted to show me, a nice certificate signed by both Joseph Orlando, president, and Harry Feinberg, secretary-treasurer, of the New York chapter of the 4th Armored Division Association, acknowledging Trump's participation as an associate grand marshal. A million four hundred thousand people had turned out for the celebration, he said, handing me some press clippings. "O.K., I see this story says a half million spectators. But, trust me, I heard a million four." Here was another clipping, from the *Times*, just the other day, confirming that rents on Fifth Avenue were the highest in the world. "And who owns more of Fifth Avenue than I do?" Or how about the new building across from the United Nations Secretariat, where he planned a "very luxurious hotel-condominium project, a major project." Who would finance it? "Any one of twenty-five different groups. They all want to finance it."

Months earlier, I'd asked Trump whom he customarily confided in during moments of tribulation. "Nobody," he said. "It's just not my thing"—a reply that didn't surprise me a bit. Salesmen, and Trump is nothing if not a brilliant salesman, specialize in simulated intimacy rather than the real thing. His modus operandi had a sharp focus: fly the flag, never budge from the premise that the universe revolves around you, and, above all, stay in character. The Trump tour de force—his evolution from rough-edged rich kid with Brooklyn and Queens political-clubhouse connections to an international name-brand commodity—remains, unmistakably, the most rewarding accomplishment of his ingenious career. The patented Trump palaver, a gaseous blather of "fantastic"s and "amazing"s and "terrific"s and "incredible"s and various synonyms for "biggest," is an indispensable ingredient of the name brand. In addition to connoting a certain quality of construction, service, and security—perhaps only Trump can explicate the meaningful distinctions between "super luxury" and "super super luxury"—his eponym subliminally suggests that a building *belongs* to him even after it's been sold off as condominiums.

Everywhere inside the Trump Organization headquarters, the walls were lined with framed magazine covers, each a shot of Trump or someone who looked an awful lot like him. The profusion of these images—of a man who possessed unusual skills, though not, evidently, a gene for irony—seemed the sum of his appetite for self-reflection. His unique talent—being "Trump" or, as he often referred to himself, "the Trumpster," looming ubiquitous by reducing himself to a persona—exempted him from introspection.

If the gossips hinted that he'd been cuckolded, they had it all wrong; untying the marital knot was based upon straightforward economics. He had a prenuptial agreement, because "if you're a person of wealth you have to have one." In the words of his attorney, Jay Goldberg, the agreement was "as solid as concrete." It would reportedly pay Marla a million dollars, plus some form of child support and alimony, and the time to do a deal was sooner rather than later. A year from now, she would become entitled to a percentage of his net worth. And, as a source *very close* to Trump made plain, "If it goes from a fixed amount to what could be a very enormous amount—even a small percentage of two and a half billion dollars or whatever is a lot of money—we're talking about very huge things. The numbers are much bigger than people understand."

The long-term matrimonial odds had never been terrifically auspicious. What was Marla Maples, after all, but a tabloid cartoon of the Other Woman, an alliteration you could throw the cliché manual at: a leggy, curvaceous blond-bombshell beauty-pageant-winning actress-model-whatever? After a couple of years of deftly choreographed love spats, Donald and Marla produced a love child, whom they could not resist naming Tiffany. A few months before they went legit, Marla told a television interviewer that the contemplation of marriage tended to induce in Donald the occasional "little freak-out" or visit from the "fear monster." Her role, she explained, was "to work with him and help him get over that fear monster." Whenever they traveled, she said, she took along her wedding dress. ("Might as well. You've got to be prepared.") The ceremony, at the Plaza Hotel, right before Christmas 1993, drew an audience of a thousand but, judging by the heavy turnout of Atlantic City high rollers, one not deemed A-list. The Trump Taj Mahal casino commemorated the occasion by issuing a Donald-and-Marla five-dollar gambling chip.

The last time around, splitting with Ivana, he'd lost the P.R. battle from the get-go. After falling an entire news cycle behind Ivana's spinmeisters, he never managed to catch up. In one ill-advised eruption, he told Liz Smith that his wife reminded him of his bête noire Leona Helmsley, and the columnist chided, "Shame on you, Donald! How dare you say that about the mother of your children?" His only moment of unadulterated, so to speak, gratification occurred when an acquaintance of Marla's blabbed about his swordsmanship. The screamer BEST SEX I'VE EVER HAD—an instant classic—is widely regarded as the most libel-proof headline ever published by the *Post*. On the surface, the coincidence of his first marital breakup with the fact that he owed a few billion he couldn't exactly pay back seemed extraordinarily unpropitious. In retrospect, his timing was *excellent.* Ivana had hoped to nullify a postnuptial agreement whose provenance could be traced to Donald's late friend and preceptor the lawyer-fixer and humanitarian Roy Cohn. Though the agreement entitled her to fourteen million dollars plus a forty-six-room house in Connecticut, she and her counsel decided to ask for half of everything Trump owned; extrapolating from Donald's blustery pronouncements over the years, they pegged her share at two and a half billion. In the end, she was forced to settle for the terms stipulated in the agreement because Donald, at that juncture, conveniently appeared to be broke.

Now, of course, according to Trump, things were much different. Business was stronger than ever. And, of course, he wanted to be fair to Marla. Only a million bucks? Hey, a deal was a deal. He meant "fair" in a larger sense: "I think it's very unfair to Marla, or, for that matter, anyone—while there are many positive things, like life style, which is at the highest level—I think it's unfair to Marla always to be subjected to somebody who enjoys his business and does it at a very high level and does it on a big scale. There are lots of compensating balances. You live in the Mar-a-Lagos of the world, you live in the best apartment. But, I think you understand, I don't have very much time. I just don't have very much time. There's nothing I can do about what I do other than stopping. And I just don't want to stop."

• • •

A securities analyst who has studied Trump's peregrinations for many years believes, "Deep down, he wants to be Madonna." In other words, to ask how the gods could have permitted Trump's resurrection is to mistake profound superficiality for profundity, performance art for serious drama. A prime example of superficiality at its most rewarding: the Trump International Hotel & Tower, a fifty-two-story hotel-condominium conversion of the former Gulf & Western Building, on Columbus Circle, which opened last January. The Trump name on the skyscraper belies the fact that his ownership is limited to his penthouse apartment and a stake in the hotel's restaurant and garage, which he received as part of his development fee. During the grand-opening ceremonies, however, such details seemed not to matter as he gave this assessment: "One of the great buildings anywhere in New York, anywhere in the world."

The festivities that day included a feng-shui ritual in the lobby, a gesture of respect to the building's high proportion of Asian buyers, who regard a Trump property as a good place to sink flight capital. An efficient schmoozer, Trump worked the room quickly—a backslap and a wink, a finger on the lapels, no more than a minute with anyone who wasn't a police commissioner, a district attorney, or a mayoral candidate—and then he was ready to go. His executive assistant, Norma Foerderer, and two other Trump Organization executives were waiting in a car to return to the office. Before it pulled away, he experienced a tug of noblesse oblige. "Hold on, just lemme say hello to these Kinney guys," he said, jumping out to greet a group of parking attendants. "Good job, fellas. You're gonna be working here for years to come." It was a quintessential Trumpian gesture, of the sort that explains his popularity among people who barely dare to dream of living in one of his creations.

Back at the office, a *Times* reporter, Michael Gordon, was on the line, calling from Moscow. Gordon had just interviewed a Russian artist named Zurab Tsereteli, a man with a sense of grandiosity familiar to Trump. Was it true, Gordon asked, that Tsereteli and Trump had discussed erecting on the Hudson River a statue of Christopher Columbus that was six feet taller than the Statue of Liberty?

"Yes, it's already been made, from what I understand," said Trump, who had met Tsereteli a couple of months earlier, in Moscow. "It's got forty million dollars' worth of bronze in it, and Zurab would like it to be at my West Side Yards development"—a seventy-five-acre tract called Riverside South—"and we are working toward that end."

According to Trump, the head had arrived in America, the rest of the body was still in Moscow, and the whole thing was being donated by the Russian government. "The mayor of Moscow has written a letter to Rudy Giuliani stating that they would like to make a gift of this great work by Zurab. It would be my honor if we could work it out with the City of New York. I am absolutely favorably disposed toward it. Zurab is a very unusual guy. This man is major and legit."

Trump hung up and said to me, "See what I do? All this bullshit. Know what? After shaking five thousand hands, I think I'll go wash mine."

Norma Foerderer, however, had some pressing business. A lecture agency in Canada was offering Trump a chance to give three speeches over three consecutive days, for seventy-five thousand dollars a pop. "Plus," she said, "they provide a private jet, secretarial services, and a weekend at a ski resort."

How did Trump feel about it?

"My attitude is if somebody's willing to pay me two hundred and twenty-five thousand dollars to make a speech, it seems stupid not to show up. You know why I'll do it? Because I don't think anyone's ever been paid that much."

Would it be fresh material?

"It'll be fresh to them."

Next item: Norma had drafted a letter to Mar-a-Lago members, inviting them to a dinner featuring a speech by George Pataki and entertainment by Marvin Hamlisch. "Oh, and speaking of the Governor, I just got a call. They're shooting a new 'I Love New York' video and they'd like Libby Pataki to go up and down our escalator. I said fine."

A Mar-a-Lago entertainment booker named Jim Grau called about a Carly Simon concert. Trump switched on his speakerphone: "Is she gonna do it?"

"Well, two things have to be done, Donald. No. 1, she'd like to hear from you. And, No. 2, she'd like to turn it in some degree into a benefit for Christopher Reeve."

"That's not a bad idea," said Trump. "Is Christopher Reeve gonna come? He can come down on my plane. So what do I have to do, call her?"

"I want to tell you how we got Carly on this because some of your friends are involved."

"Jim, I don't give a shit. Who the hell cares?"

"Please, Donald. Remember when you had your yacht up there? You had Rose Styron aboard. And her husband wrote *Sophie's Choice*. And it's through her good offices—"

"O.K. Good. So thank 'em and maybe invite 'em." Click.

"Part of my problem," Trump said to me, "is that I have to do a lot of things myself. It takes so much time. Julio Iglesias is coming to Mar-a-Lago, but I have to *call* Julio, I have to have *lunch* with Julio. I have Pavarotti coming. Pavarotti doesn't perform for anybody. He's the highest-paid performer in the world. A million dollars a performance. The hardest guy to get. If I call him, he'll do it—for a *huge* amount less. Why? Because they like me, they respect me, I don't know."

. . .

During Trump's ascendancy, in the 1980s, the essence of his performance art—an opera-buffa parody of wealth—accounted for his populist appeal as well as for the opprobrium of those who regard with distaste the spectacle of an unbridled id. Delineating his commercial aesthetic, he once told an interviewer, "I have glitzy casinos because people expect it. . . . Glitz works in Atlantic City. . . . And in my residential buildings I sometimes use flash, which is a level below glitz." His first monument to himself, Trump Tower, on Fifth Avenue at Fifty-sixth Street, which opened its doors in 1984, possessed many genuinely impressive elements—a sixty-eight-story sawtoothed silhouette, a salmon-colored Italian-marble atrium equipped with an eighty-foot waterfall—and became an instant tourist attraction. In Atlantic City, the idea was to slather on as much ornamentation as possible, the goal being (a) to titillate with the fantasy that a Trump-like life was a lifelike life and (b) to distract from the fact that he'd lured you inside to pick your pocket.

At times, neither glitz nor flash could disguise financial reality. A story in the *Times* three months ago contained a reference to his past "brush with bankruptcy," and Trump, though gratified that the *Times* gave him play on the front page, took umbrage at that phrase. He "never went bankrupt," he wrote in a letter to the editor, nor did he "ever, at any time, come close." Having triumphed over adversity, Trump assumes the prerogative to write history.

In fact, by 1990, he was not only at risk, he was, by any rational standard, hugely in the red. Excessively friendly bankers infected with the promiscuous optimism that made the '80s so memorable and so forgettable had financed Trump's acquisitive impulses to the tune of three billion seven hundred and fifty million dollars. The personally guaranteed portion—almost a billion—represented the value of Trump's good will, putative creditworthiness, and capacity for shame. A debt restructuring began in the spring of 1990 and continued for several years. In the process, six hundred or seven hundred or perhaps eight hundred million of his creditors' dollars vaporized and drifted wherever lost money goes. In America, there is no such thing as a debtors' prison, nor is there a tidy moral to this story.

Several of Trump's trophies—the Plaza Hotel and all three Atlantic City casinos—were subjected to "prepackaged bankruptcy," an efficiency maneuver that is less costly than the full-blown thing. Because the New Jersey Casino Control Act requires "financial stability" for a gaming license, it seems hard to avoid the inference that Trump's Atlantic City holdings were in serious jeopardy. Nevertheless, "blip" is the alternative "b" word he prefers, as in "So the market, as you know, turns lousy and I have this blip."

Trump began plotting his comeback before the rest of the world—or, perhaps, even he—fully grasped the direness of his situation. In April of 1990, he announced to the *Wall Street Journal* a plan to sell certain assets and become the "king of cash," a stratagem that would supposedly set the stage for a shrewd campaign of bargain hunting. That same month, he drew down the final twenty-five million dollars of an unsecured hundred-million-dollar personal line of credit from Bankers Trust. Within seven weeks, he failed to deliver a forty-three-million-dollar payment due to bondholders of the Trump Castle Casino, and he also missed a thirty-million-dollar interest payment to one of the estimated hundred and fifty banks that were concerned about his well-being. An army of bankruptcy lawyers began camping out in various boardrooms.

Making the blip go away entailed, among other sacrifices, forfeiting management control of the Plaza and handing over the titles to the Trump Shuttle (the old Eastern Airlines Boston–New York–Washington route) and a twin-towered thirty-two-story condominium building near West Palm Beach, Florida. He also said good-bye to his two-hundred-and-eighty-two-foot yacht, the *Trump Princess*, and to his Boeing 727. Appraisers inventoried the contents of his Trump Tower homestead. Liens were attached to just about everything but his Brioni suits. Perhaps the ultimate indignity was having to agree to a personal spending cap of four hundred and fifty thousand dollars a month.

• • •

It would have been tactically wise, to say nothing of tactful, if, as Trump's creditors wrote off large chunks of their portfolios, he could have curbed his breathtaking propensity for self-aggrandizement. The bravado diminished somewhat for a couple of years—largely because the press stopped paying attention—but by 1993 he was proclaiming, "This year has been the most successful year I've had in business." Every year since, he's issued the same news flash. A spate of Trump-comeback articles appeared in 1996, including several timed to coincide with his fiftieth birthday.

Then, last October, Trump came into possession of what a normal person would regard as real money. For a hundred and forty-two million dollars, he sold his half interest in the Grand Hyatt Hotel, on Forty-second Street, to the Pritzker family, of Chicago, his longtime, and long-estranged, partners in the property. Most of the proceeds weren't his to keep, but he walked away with more than twenty-five million dollars. The chief significance of the Grand Hyatt sale was that it enabled Trump to extinguish the remnants of his once monstrous personally guaranteed debt. When *Forbes* published its annual list of the four hundred richest Americans, he sneaked on (three hundred and seventy-third position) with an estimated net worth of four hundred and fifty million. Trump, meanwhile, had compiled his own unaudited appraisal, one he was willing to share along with the amusing caveat "I've never shown this to a reporter before." According to his calculations, he was actually worth two and a quarter billion dollars—*Forbes* had lowballed him by eighty percent. Still, he had officially rejoined the plutocracy, his first appearance since the blip.

Jay Goldberg, who in addition to handling Trump's matrimonial legal matters also represented him in the Grand Hyatt deal, told me that, after it closed, his client confessed that the novelty of being unencumbered had him lying awake nights. When I asked Trump about this, he said, "Leverage is an amazing phenomenon. I love leverage. Plus, I've never been a huge sleeper." Trump doesn't drink or smoke, claims he's never even had a cup of coffee. He functions, evidently, according to inverse logic and metabolism. What most people would find unpleasantly stimulating—owing vastly more than you should to lenders who, figuratively, at least, can carve you into small pieces—somehow engenders in him a soothing narcotic effect. That, in any event, is the impression Trump seeks to convey, though the point is now moot. Bankers, typically not the most perspicacious species on earth, from time to time get religion, and there aren't many who will soon be lining up to thrust fresh bazillions at him.

. . .

When I met with Trump for the first time, several months ago, he set out to acquaint me with facts that, to his consternation, had remained stubbornly hidden from the public. Several times, he uttered the phrase "off the record, but you can use it." I understood the implication—I was his tool—but failed to see the purpose. "If you have me saying these things, even though they're true, I sound like a schmuck," he explained. How to account, then, for the bombast of the previous two decades? Alair Townsend, a former deputy mayor in the Koch administration, once quipped, "I wouldn't believe Donald Trump if his tongue were notarized." In time, this bon mot became misattributed to Leona Helmsley, who was only too happy to claim authorship. Last fall, after Evander Holyfield upset Mike Tyson in a heavyweight title fight, Trump snookered the *News* into reporting that he'd collected twenty million bucks by betting a million on the underdog. This prompted the *Post* to make calls to some Las Vegas bookies, who confirmed—shockingly!—that nobody had been handling that kind of action or laying odds close to 20-1. Trump never blinked, just moved on to the next bright idea.

"I don't think people know how big my business is," Trump told me. "Somehow, they know Trump the celebrity. But I'm the biggest developer in New York. And I'm the biggest there is in the casino business. And that's pretty good to be the biggest in both. So that's a lot of stuff." He talked about 40 Wall Street—"truly one of the most beautiful buildings in New York"—a seventy-two-story landmark that he was renovating. He said he owned the new Niketown store, tucked under Trump Tower; there was a deal to convert the Mayfair Hotel, at Sixty-fifth and Park, into "super-super-luxury apartments . . . but that's like a small one." He owned the land under the Ritz-Carlton, on Central Park South. ("That's a little thing. Nobody knows that I own that. In that way, I'm not really understood.") With CBS, he now owned the

Miss U.S.A., Miss Teen U.S.A., and Miss Universe beauty pageants. He pointed to a stack of papers on his desk, closing documents for the Trump International Hotel & Tower. "Look at these contracts. I get these to sign every day. I've signed hundreds of these. Here's a contract for two-point-two million dollars. It's a building that isn't even opened yet. It's eighty-three percent sold, and nobody even knows it's there. For each contract, I need to sign twenty-two times, and if you think that's easy ... You know, all the buyers want my signature. I had someone else who works for me signing, and at the closings the buyers got angry. I told myself, 'You know, these people are paying a million eight, a million seven, two million nine, four million one—for those kinds of numbers, I'll sign the fucking contract.' I understand. Fuck it. It's just more work."

As a real-estate impresario, Trump certainly has no peer. His assertion that he is the biggest real-estate *developer* in New York, however, presumes an elastic definition of that term. Several active developers— among them the Rudins, the Roses, the Milsteins— have added more residential and commercial space to the Manhattan market and have historically held

on to what they built. When the outer boroughs figure in the tally—and if Donald isn't allowed to claim
credit for the middle-income high-rise rental projects
that generated the fortune amassed by his ninety-one-
year-old father, Fred—he slips further in the rank-
ings. But if one's standard of comparison is simply the
number of buildings that bear the developer's name,
Donald dominates the field. Trump's vaunted art of
the deal has given way to the art of "image ownership." By appearing to exert control over assets that
aren't necessarily his—at least not in ways that his
pronouncements suggest—he exercises his real talent:
using his name as a form of leverage. "It's German in
derivation," he has said. "Nobody really knows where
it came from. It's very unusual, but it just is a good
name to have."

In the Trump International Hotel & Tower make-
over, his role is, in effect, that of broker-promoter
rather than risktaker. In 1993, the General Electric
Pension Trust, which took over the building in a fore-
closure, hired the Galbreath Company, an international real-estate management firm, to recommend
how to salvage its mortgage on a nearly empty skyscraper that had an annoying tendency to sway in

the wind. Along came Trump, proposing a three-way joint venture. G.E. would put up all the money—two hundred and seventy-five million dollars—and Trump and Galbreath would provide expertise. The market timing proved remarkably favorable. When Trump totted up the profits and calculated that his share came to more than forty million bucks, self-restraint eluded him, and he took out advertisements announcing "The Most Successful Condominium Tower Ever Built in the United States."

A minor specimen of his image ownership is his ballyhooed "half interest" in the Empire State Building, which he acquired in 1994. Trump's initial investment—not a dime—matches his apparent return thus far. His partners, the illegitimate daughter and disreputable son-in-law of an even more disreputable Japanese billionaire named Hideki Yokoi, seem to have paid forty million dollars for the building, though their title, even on a sunny day, is somewhat clouded. Under the terms of leases executed in 1961, the building is operated by a partnership controlled by Peter Malkin and the estate of the late Harry Helmsley. The lessees receive almost ninety million dollars a year from the building's tenants but are required to pay the lessors (Trump's partners) only about a million nine hundred thousand. Trump himself doesn't share in these proceeds, and the leases don't expire until 2076. Only if he can devise a way to break the leases will his "ownership" acquire any value. His strategy—suing the Malkin-Helmsley group for a hundred million dollars, alleging, among other things, that they've violated the leases by allowing the building to become a "rodent infested" commercial slum—has proved fruitless. In February, when an armed madman on the eighty-sixth-floor observation deck killed a sightseer and wounded six others before shooting himself, it seemed a foregone conclusion that Trump, ever vigilant, would exploit the tragedy, and he did not disappoint. "Leona Helmsley should be ashamed of herself," he told the *Post*.

One day, when I was in Trump's office, he took a phone call from an investment banker, an opaque conversation that, after he hung up, I asked him to elucidate.

"Whatever complicates the world more I do," he said.

Come again?

"It's always good to do things nice and complicated so that nobody can figure it out."

Case in point: The widely held perception is that Trump is the sole visionary and master builder of Riverside South, the mega-development planned for the former Penn Central Yards, on the West Side. Trump began pawing at the property in 1974, obtained a formal option in 1977, allowed it to lapse in 1979, and re-entered the picture in 1984, when Chase Manhattan lent him eighty-four million dollars for land-purchase and development expenses. In the years that followed, he trotted out several elephantine proposals, diverse and invariably overly dense residential and commercial mixtures. "Zoning for me is a life process," Trump told me. "Zoning is something I have done and ultimately always get because people appreciate what I'm asking for and they know it's going to be the highest quality." In fact, the consensus among the West Side neighbors who studied Trump's designs was that they did not appreciate what he was asking for. An exotically banal hundred-and-fifty-story phallus—"The World's Tallest Building"—provided the centerpiece of his most vilified scheme.

The oddest passage in this byzantine history began in the late eighties, when an assortment of high-minded civic groups united to oppose Trump, enlisted their own architects, and drafted a greatly scaled-back alternative plan. The civic groups hoped to persuade Chase Manhattan, which held Trump's mortgage, to help them entice a developer who could wrest the property from their nemesis. To their dismay, and sheepish amazement, they discovered that one developer was willing to pursue their design: Trump. Over time, the so-called civic alternative has become, in the public mind, thanks to Trump's drumbeating, *his* proposal; he has appropriated conceptual ownership.

Three years ago, a syndicate of Asian investors, led by Henry Cheng, of Hong Kong's New World Development Company, assumed the task of arranging construction financing. This transaction altered Trump's involvement to a glorified form of sweat equity; for a fee paid by the investment syndicate, Trump Organization staff people would collaborate with a team from New World, monitoring the construction already under way and working on designs, zoning, and planning for the phases to come. Only when New World has recovered its investment, plus interest, will Trump begin to see any real profit—twenty-five years, at least, after he first cast his covetous eye at the Penn Central rail yards. According to Trump's unaudited net-worth statement, which identifies Riverside South as "Trump Boulevard," he "owns 30–50% of the project, depending on performance." This "ownership," however, is a potential profit share rather than actual equity. Six hundred million dollars is the value Trump imputes to this highly provisional asset.

• • •

Of course, the "comeback" Trump is much the same as the Trump of the '80s; there is no "new" Trump, just as there was never a "new" Nixon. Rather, all along there have been several Trumps: the hyperbole addict who prevaricates for fun and profit; the knowledgeable builder whose associates profess awe at his attention to detail; the narcissist whose self-absorption doesn't account for his dead-on ability to exploit other people's weaknesses; the perpetual seventeen-year-old* who lives in a zero-sum world of winners and "total losers," loyal friends and "complete scumbags"; the insatiable publicity hound who courts the press on a daily basis and, when he doesn't like what he reads, attacks the messengers as "human garbage"; the chairman and largest stockholder of a billion-dollar public corporation who seems unable to resist heralding overly optimistic earnings projections, which then fail to materialize, thereby eroding the value of his investment—in sum, a fellow both slippery and naïve, artfully calculating and recklessly heedless of consequences.

Trump's most caustic detractors in New York real-estate circles disparage him as "a casino operator in New Jersey," as if to say, "He's not really even one of us." Such derision is rooted in resentment that his rescue from oblivion—his strategy for remaining the marketable real-estate commodity "Trump"—hinged upon his ability to pump cash out of Atlantic City. The Trump image is nowhere more concentrated than in

* Recent events have shown conclusively that my characterization of Trump's behavioral age was overly generous by at least ten years. Mea culpa.

Atlantic City, and it is there, of late, that the Trump alchemy—transforming other people's money into his own wealth—has been most strenuously tested.

To bail himself out with the banks, Trump converted his casinos to public ownership, despite the fact that the constraints inherent in answering to shareholders do not come to him naturally. Inside the Trump Organization, for instance, there is talk of "the Donald factor," the three to five dollars per share that Wall Street presumably discounts Trump Hotels & Casino Resorts by allowing for his braggadocio and unpredictability. The initial public offering, in June 1995, raised a hundred and forty million dollars, at fourteen dollars a share. Less than a year later, a secondary offering, at thirty-one dollars per share, brought in an additional three hundred and eighty million dollars. Trump's personal stake in the company now stands at close to forty percent. As chairman, Donald had an excellent year in 1996, drawing a million-dollar salary, another million for miscellaneous "services," and a bonus of five million. As a shareholder, however, he did considerably less well. A year ago, the stock traded at thirty-five dollars; it now sells for around ten.

Notwithstanding Trump's insistence that things have never been better, Trump Hotels & Casino Resorts has to cope with several thorny liabilities, starting with a junk-bond debt load of a billion seven hundred million dollars. In 1996, the company's losses amounted to three dollars and twenty-seven cents per share—attributable, in part, to extraordinary expenses but also to the fact that the Atlantic City gaming industry has all but stopped growing. And, most glaringly, there was the burden of the Trump Castle, which experienced a ten percent revenue decline, the worst of any casino in Atlantic City.

Last October, the Castle, a heavily leveraged consistent money loser that had been wholly owned by Trump, was bought into Trump Hotels, a transaction that gave him five million eight hundred and thirty-seven thousand shares of stock. Within two weeks—helped along by a reduced earnings estimate from a leading analyst—the stock price, which had been eroding since the spring, began to slide more precipitously, triggering a shareholder lawsuit that accused Trump of self-dealing and a "gross breach of his fiduciary duties." At which point he began looking for a partner. The deal Trump came up with called for

Colony Capital, a sharp real-estate outfit from Los Angeles, to buy fifty-one percent of the Castle for a price that seemed to vindicate the terms under which he'd unloaded it on the public company. Closer inspection revealed, however, that Colony's capital injection would give it high-yield preferred, rather than common, stock—in other words, less an investment than a loan. Trump-l'oeil: Instead of trying to persuade the world that he owned something that wasn't his, he was trying to convey the impression that he would part with an onerous asset that, as a practical matter, he would still be stuck with. In any event, in March the entire deal fell apart. Trump, in character, claimed that he, not Colony, had called it off.

The short-term attempt to solve the Castle's problems is a four-million-dollar cosmetic overhaul. This so-called re-theming will culminate in June, when the casino acquires a new name: Trump Marina. One day this winter, I accompanied Trump when he buzzed into Atlantic City for a re-theming meeting with Nicholas Ribis, the president and chief executive officer of Trump Hotels, and several Castle executives. The discussion ranged from the size of the lettering on the outside of the building to the sparkling gray granite in the lobby to potential future renderings, including a version with an as yet unbuilt hotel tower and a permanently docked yacht to be called *Miss Universe.* Why the boat? "It's just an attraction," Trump said. "You understand, this would be part of a phase-two or phase-three expansion. It's going to be the largest yacht in the world."

From the re-theming meeting, we headed for the casino, and along the way Trump received warm salutations. A white-haired woman wearing a pink warmup suit and carrying a bucket of quarters said, "Mr. Trump, I just love you, darling." He replied, "Thank you. I love you, too," then turned to me and said, "You see, they're good people. And I like people. You've gotta be nice. They're like friends."

The Castle had two thousand two hundred and thirty-nine slot machines, including, in a far corner, thirteen brand-new and slightly terrifying *Wheel of Fortune*–theme contraptions, which were about to be officially unveiled. On hand were representatives of International Game Technology (the machines' manufacturer), a press entourage worthy of a military briefing in the wake of a Grenada-caliber invasion, and a couple of hundred onlookers—all drawn by the prospect of a personal appearance by Vanna White, the doyenne of *Wheel of Fortune*. Trump's arrival generated satisfying expressions of awe from the rubberneckers, though not the spontaneous burst of applause that greeted Vanna, who had been conscripted for what was described as "the ceremonial first pull."

When Trump spoke, he told the gathering, "This is the beginning of a new generation of machine." Vanna pulled the crank, but the crush of reporters made it impossible to tell what was going on or even what denomination of currency had been sacrificed. The demographics of the crowd suggested that the most efficient machine would be one that permitted direct deposit of a Social Security check. After a delay that featured a digital musical cacophony, the machine spat back a few coins. Trump said, "Ladies and gentlemen, it took a little while. We hope it doesn't take you as long. And we just want to thank you for being our friends." And then we were out of there. "This is what we do. What can I tell you?" Trump said, as we made our way through the casino.

Vanna White was scheduled to join us for the helicopter flight back to New York, and later, as we swung over Long Island City, heading for a heliport on the East Side, Trump gave Vanna a little hug and, not for the first time, praised her star turn at the Castle. "For the opening of thirteen slot machines, I'd say we did all right today," he said, and then they slapped high fives.

• • •

In a 1990 *Playboy* interview, Trump said that the yacht, the glitzy casinos, the gleaming bronze of Trump Tower were all "props for the show," adding that "the show is 'Trump' and it is sold-out performances everywhere." In 1985, the show moved to Palm Beach. For ten million dollars, Trump bought Mar-a-Lago, a hundred-and-eighteen-room Hispano-Moorish-Venetian castle built in the '20s by Marjorie Merriweather Post and E. F. Hutton, set on seventeen and a half acres extending from the ocean to Lake Worth. Ever since, his meticulous restoration and literal regilding of the property have been a work in progress. The winter of 1995–96 was Mar-a-Lago's first full season as a commercial venture, a private club with a twenty-five-thousand-dollar initiation fee (which later rose to fifty thousand and is now quoted at seventy-five thousand). The combination of the Post-Hutton pedigree and Trump's stewardship offered a paradigm of how an aggressively enterprising devotion to Good Taste inevitably transmutes to Bad Taste—but might nevertheless pay for itself.

Only Trump and certain of his minions know who among Mar-a-Lago's more than three hundred listed members has actually forked over initiation fees and who's paid how much for the privilege. Across the years, there have been routine leaks by a mysterious unnamed spokesman within the Trump Organization to the effect that this or that member of the British Royal Family was planning to buy a pied-à-terre in Trump Tower. It therefore came as no surprise when, during early recruiting efforts at Mar-a-Lago, Trump announced that the Prince and Princess of Wales, their mutual antipathy notwithstanding, had signed up. Was there any documentation? Well, um, Chuck and Di were *honorary* members. Among the honorary members who have yet to pass through Mar-a-Lago's portals are Henry Kissinger and Elizabeth Taylor.

The most direct but not exactly most serene way to travel to Mar-a-Lago, I discovered one weekend not long ago, is aboard Trump's 727, the same aircraft he gave up during the blip and, after an almost decent interval, bought back. My fellow-passengers included Eric Javits, a lawyer and nephew of the late Senator Jacob Javits, bumming a ride; Ghislaine Maxwell, the daughter of the late publishing tycoon and inadequate swimmer Robert Maxwell, also bumming a ride; Matthew Calamari, a telephone-booth-size body-guard who is the head of security for the entire Trump Organization; and Eric Trump, Donald's thirteen-year-old son.

The solid-gold fixtures and hardware (sinks, seat-belt clasps, door hinges, screws), well-stocked bar and larder, queen-size bed, and bidet (easily outfitted with a leather-cushioned cover in case of sudden tur-bulence) implied hedonistic possibilities—the plane often ferried high rollers to Atlantic City—but I wit-nessed only good clean fun. We hadn't been airborne long when Trump decided to watch a movie. He'd brought along *Michael*, a recent release, but twenty minutes after popping it into the VCR he got bored and switched to an old favorite, a Jean-Claude Van Damme slugfest called *Bloodsport*, which he pro-nounced "an incredible, fantastic movie." By assigning to his son the task of fast-forwarding through all the plot exposition—Trump's goal being "to get this two-hour movie down to forty-five minutes"—he eliminated any lulls between the nose hammering, kidney tenderizing, and shin whacking. When a beefy bad guy who was about to squish a normal-sized good guy received a crippling blow to the scrotum, I laughed. "Admit it, you're laughing!" Trump shouted. "You want to write that Donald Trump was loving this ridiculous Jean-Claude Van Damme movie, but are you willing to put in there that you were loving it, too?"

A small convoy of limousines greeted us on the runway in Palm Beach, and during the ten-minute drive to Mar-a-Lago Trump waxed enthusiastic about a "spectacular, world-class" golf course he was planning to build on county-owned land directly opposite the airport. Trump, by the way, is a skilled golfer. A source extremely close to him—by which I mean off the record, but I can use it—told me that Claude Harmon, a former winner of the Masters tournament and for thirty-three years the club pro at Winged Foot, in Mamaroneck, New York, once described Donald as "the best weekend player" he'd ever seen.

The only formal event on Trump's agenda had already got under way. Annually, the publisher of *Forbes* invites eleven corporate potentates to Florida, where they spend a couple of nights aboard the company yacht, the *Highlander*, and, during the day, adroitly palpate each other's brains and size up each other's short games. A supplementary group of capital-gains-tax skeptics had been invited to a Friday-night banquet in the Mar-a-Lago ballroom. Trump arrived between the roast-duck appetizer and the roasted-portabello-mushroom salad and took his seat next to Malcolm S. (Steve) Forbes, Jr., the erstwhile Presidential candidate and the chief executive of *Forbes,* at a table that also included *les grands fromages* of Hertz, Merrill Lynch, the C.I.T. Group, and Countrywide Credit Industries. At an adjacent table, Marla Maples Trump, who had just returned from Shreveport, Louisiana, where she was rehearsing her role as co-host of the Miss U.S.A. pageant, discussed global politics and the sleeping habits of three-year-old Tiffany with the corporate chiefs and chief spouses of AT&T, Sprint, and Office Depot. During coffee, Donald assured everyone present that they were "very special" to him, that he wanted them to think of Mar-a-Lago as home, and that they were all welcome to drop by the spa the next day for a freebie.

Tony Senecal, a former mayor of Martinsburg, West Virginia, who now doubles as Trump's butler and Mar-a-Lago's resident historian, told me, "Some of the restoration work that's being done here is so subtle it's almost not Trump-like." Subtlety, however, is not the dominant motif. Weary from handling Trump's legal work, Jay Goldberg used to retreat with his wife to Mar-a-Lago for a week each year. Never mind the tapestries, murals, frescoes, winged statuary, life-size portrait of Trump (titled *The Visionary*), bathtub-size flower-filled samovars, vaulted Corinthian colonnade, thirty-four-foot ceilings, blinding chandeliers, marquetry, overstuffed and gold-leaf-stamped everything else, Goldberg told me; what nudged him around the bend was a small piece of fruit.

"We were surrounded by a staff of twenty people," he said, "including a footman. I didn't even know what that was. I thought maybe a chiropodist. Anyway, wherever I turned there was always a bowl of fresh fruit. So there I am, in our room, and I decide to step into the bathroom to take a leak. And on the way

I grab a kumquat and eat it. Well, by the time I come out of the bathroom the *kumquat has been replaced*."

As for the Mar-a-Lago spa, aerobic exercise is an activity Trump indulges in "as little as possible," and he's therefore chosen not to micromanage its daily affairs. Instead, he brought in a Texas outfit called the Greenhouse Spa, proven specialists in mud wraps, manual lymphatic drainage, reflexology, shiatsu and Hawaiian hot-rock massage, loofah polishes, sea-salt rubs, aromatherapy, acupuncture, peat baths, and Japanese steeping-tub protocol. Evidently, Trump's philosophy of wellness is rooted in a belief that prolonged exposure to exceptionally attractive young female spa attendants will instill in the male clientele a will to live. Accordingly, he limits his role to a pocket veto of key hiring decisions. While giving me a tour of the main exercise room, where Tony Bennett, who does a couple of gigs at Mar-a-Lago each season and has been designated an "artist-in-residence," was taking a brisk walk on a treadmill, Trump introduced me to "our resident physician, Dr. Ginger Lea Southall"—a recent chiropractic-college graduate. As Dr. Ginger, out of earshot, manipulated the sore back of a grateful member, I asked Trump where she had done her training. "I'm not sure," he said. "Bay-watch Medical School? Does that sound right? I'll tell you the truth. Once I saw Dr. Ginger's photograph, I didn't really need to look at her résumé or anyone else's. Are you asking, 'Did we hire her because she'd trained at Mount Sinai for fifteen years?' The answer is no. And I'll tell you why: because by the time she's spent fifteen years at Mount Sinai, we don't want to look at her."

· · ·

My visit happened to coincide with the coldest weather of the winter, and this gave me a convenient excuse, at frequent intervals, to retreat to my thousand-dollar-a-night suite and huddle under the bedcovers in fetal position. Which is where I was around ten-thirty Saturday night, when I got a call from Tony Senecal, summoning me to the ballroom. The furnishings had been altered since the *Forbes* banquet the previous evening. Now there was just a row of armchairs in the center of the room and a couple of low tables, an arrangement that meant Donald and Marla were get-ting ready for a late dinner in front of the TV. They'd already been out to a movie with Eric and Tiffany and some friends and bodyguards, and now a theater-size screen had descended from the ceiling so that they could watch a pay-per-view telecast of a junior-welterweight-championship boxing match between Oscar De La Hoya and Miguel Angel Gonzalez.

Marla was eating something green, while Donald had ordered his favorite, meat loaf and mashed potatoes. "We have a chef who makes the greatest meat loaf in the world," he said. "It's so great I told him to put it on the menu. So whenever we have it, half the people order it. But then afterward, if you ask them what they ate, they always deny it."

Trump is not only a boxing fan but an occasional promoter, and big bouts are regularly staged at his hotels in Atlantic City. Whenever he shows up in person, he drops by to wish the fighters luck beforehand and is always accorded a warm welcome, with the exception of a chilly reception not long ago from the idiosyncratic Polish head-butter and rabbit-puncher Andrew Golota. This was just before Golota went out and pounded Riddick Bowe into retirement, only to get himself disqualified for a series of low blows that would've been perfectly legal in *Bloodsport*.

"Golota's a killer," Trump said admiringly. "A stone-cold killer."

When I asked Marla how she felt about boxing, she said, "I enjoy it a lot, just as long as nobody gets hurt."

• • •

When a call came a while back from Aleksandr Ivanovich Lebed, the retired general, amateur boxer, and restless pretender to the Presidency of Russia, explaining that he was headed to New York and wanted to arrange a meeting, Trump was pleased but not surprised. The list of superpower leaders and geopolitical strategists with whom Trump has engaged in frank and fruitful exchanges of viewpoints includes Mikhail Gorbachev, Richard Nixon, Jimmy Carter, Ronald Reagan, George Bush, former Secretary of Defense William Perry, and the entire Joint Chiefs of Staff. (He's also pals with Sylvester Stallone and Clint Eastwood, men's men who enjoy international reputations for racking up massive body counts.) In 1987, fresh from his grandest public-relations coup—repairing in three and a half months, under budget and for no fee, the Wollman skating rink in Central Park, a job that the city of New York had spent six years and twelve million dollars bungling—Trump contemplated how, in a larger sphere, he could advertise himself as a doer and dealmaker. One stunt involved orchestrating an "invitation" from the federal government to examine the Williamsburg Bridge, which was falling apart. Trump had no real interest in the job, but by putting on a hard hat and taking a stroll on the bridge for the cameras he stoked the fantasy that he could rebuild the city's entire infrastructure. From there it was only a short leap to saving the planet. What if, say, a troublemaker like Muammar Qaddafi got his hands on a nuclear arsenal? Well, Trump declared, he stood ready to work with the leaders of the then Soviet Union to coordinate a formula for coping with Armageddon-minded lunatics.

The clear purpose of Lebed's trip to America, an unofficial visit that coincided with the second Clinton Inaugural, was to add some reassuring human texture to his image as a plainspoken tough guy. Simultaneously, his domestic political prospects could be enhanced if voters back home got the message that Western capitalists felt comfortable with him. Somewhere in Lebed's calculations was the understanding that, to the nouveau entrepreneurs of the freebooter's paradise that is now Russia, Trump looked and smelled like very old money.

Their rendezvous was scheduled for midmorning. Having enlisted as an interpreter Inga Bogutska, a receptionist whose father, by coincidence, was a Russian general, Trump decided to greet his visitor in the lobby. When it turned out that Lebed, en route from an audience with a group of *Times* editors and reporters, was running late, Trump occupied himself by practicing his golf swing and surveying the female pedestrians in the atrium. Finally, Lebed arrived, a middle-aged but ageless fellow with a weathered, fleshy face and hooded eyes, wearing a gray business suit and an impassive expression. After posing for a *Times* photographer, they rode an elevator to the twenty-sixth floor, and along the way Trump asked, "So, how is everything in New York?"

"Well, it's hard to give an assessment, but I think it is brilliant," Lebed replied. He had a deep, bull-froggy voice, and his entourage of a half-dozen men included an interpreter, who rendered Inga Bogutska superfluous.

"Yes, it's been doing very well," Trump agreed. "New York is on a very strong up. And we've been reading a lot of great things about this gentleman and his country."

Inside his office, Trump immediately began sharing with Lebed some of his treasured possessions. "This is a shoe that was given to me by Shaquille O'Neal," he said. "Basketball. *Shaquille O'Neal*. Seven feet three inches, I guess. This is his sneaker, the actual sneaker. In fact, he gave this to me after a game."

"I've always said," Lebed sagely observed, "that after size 45, which I wear, then you start wearing trunks on your feet."

"That's true," said Trump. He moved on to a replica of a Mike Tyson heavyweight-championship belt, followed by an Evander Holyfield glove. "He gave me this on my fiftieth birthday. And then he beat Tyson. I didn't know who to root for. And then, again, here is Shaquille O'Neal's shirt. Here, you might want to see this. This was part of an advertisement for Versace, the fashion designer. These are photographs of Madonna on the stairs at Mar-a-Lago, my house in Florida. And this photograph shows something that we just finished and are very proud of. It's a big hotel called Trump International. And it's been very successful. So we've had a lot of fun."

Trump introduced Lebed to Howard Lorber, who had accompanied him a few months earlier on his journey to Moscow, where they looked at properties to which the Trump moniker might be appended. "Howard has major investments in Russia," he told Lebed, but when Lorber itemized various ventures none seemed to ring a bell.

"See, they don't know you," Trump told Lorber. "With all that investment, they don't know you. Trump they know."

Some "poisonous people" at the *Times*, Lebed informed Trump, were "spreading some funny rumors that you are going to cram Moscow with casinos."

Laughing, Trump said, "Is that right?"

"I told them that I know you build skyscrapers in New York. High-quality skyscrapers."

"We are actually looking at something in Moscow right now, and it would be skyscrapers and hotels, not casinos. Only quality stuff. But thank you for defending me. I'll soon be going again to Moscow. We're looking at the Moskva Hotel. We're also looking at the Rossiya. That's a very big project; I think it's the largest hotel in the world. And we're working with the local government, the mayor of Moscow and the mayor's people. So far, they've been very responsive."

LEBED: "You must be a very confident person. You are building straight into the center."

TRUMP: "I always go into the center."

LEBED: "I hope I'm not offending by saying this, but I think you are a litmus testing paper. You are at the end of the edge. If Trump goes to Moscow, I think America will follow. So I consider these projects of yours to be very important. And I'd like to help you as best I can in putting your projects into life. I want to create a canal or riverbed for capital flow. I want to minimize the risks and get rid of situations where the entrepreneur has to try to hide his head between his shoulders. I told the *New York Times* I was talking to you because you are a professional—a high-level professional—and if you invest, you invest in real stuff. Serious, high-quality projects. And you deal with serious people. And I deem you to be a very serious person. That's why I'm meeting you."

TRUMP: "Well, that's very nice. Thank you very much. I have something for you. This is a little token of my respect. I hope you like it. This is a book called *The Art of the Deal*, which a lot of people have read. And if you read this book you'll know the art of the deal better than I do."

The conversation turned to Lebed's lunch arrangements and travel logistics—"It's very tiring to meet so many people," he confessed—and the dialogue began to feel stilted, as if Trump's limitations as a Kremlinologist had exhausted the potential topics. There was, however, one more subject he wanted to cover.

"Now, you were a boxer, right?" he said. "We have a lot of big matches at my hotels. We just had a match between Riddick Bowe and Andrew Golota, from Poland, who won the fight but was disqualified. He's actually a great fighter if he can ever get through a match without being disqualified. And, to me, you look tougher than Andrew Golota."

In response, Lebed pressed an index finger to his nose, or what was left of it, and flattened it against his face.

"You do look seriously tough," Trump continued. "Were you an Olympic boxer?"

"No, I had a rather modest career."

"Really? The newspapers said you had a great career."

"At a certain point, my company leader put the question straight: either you do the sports or you do the military service. And I selected the military."

"You made the right decision," Trump agreed, as if putting to rest any notion he might have entertained about promoting a Lebed exhibition bout in Atlantic City.

Norma Foerderer came in with a camera to snap a few shots for the Trump archives and to congratulate the general for his fancy footwork in Chechnya. Phone numbers were exchanged, and Lebed, before departing, offered Trump a benediction: "You leave on the earth a very good trace for centuries. We're all mortal, but the things you build will stay forever. You've already proven wrong the assertion that the higher the attic, the more trash there is."

When Trump returned from escorting Lebed to the elevator, I asked him his impressions.

"First of all, you wouldn't want to play nuclear

weapons with this fucker," he said. "Does he look as tough and cold as you've ever seen? This is not like your average real-estate guy who's rough and mean. This guy's beyond that. You see it in the eyes. This guy is a killer. How about when I asked, 'Were you a boxer?' Whoa—that nose is a piece of rubber. But me he liked. When we went out to the elevator, he was grabbing me, holding me, he felt very good. And he liked what I do. You know what? I think I did a good job for the country today."

The phone rang—Jesse Jackson calling about some office space Trump had promised to help the Rainbow Coalition lease at 40 Wall Street. ("Hello, Jesse. How ya doin'? You were on Rosie's show? She's terrific, right? Yeah, I think she is. . . . Okay-y-y, how are *you*?") Trump hung up, sat forward, his eyebrows arched, smiling a smile that contained equal measures of surprise and self-satisfaction. "You gotta say, I cover the gamut. Does the kid cover the gamut? Boy, it never ends. I mean, people have no idea. Cool life. You know, it's sort of a cool life."

. . .

One Saturday this winter, Trump and I had an appointment at Trump Tower. After I'd waited ten minutes, the concierge directed me to the penthouse. When I emerged from the elevator, there Donald stood, wearing a black cashmere topcoat, navy suit, blue-and-white pin-striped shirt, and maroon necktie. "I thought you might like to see my apartment," he said, and as I squinted against the glare of gilt and mirrors in the entrance corridor he added, "I don't really do this." That we both knew this to be a transparent fib—photo spreads of the fifty-three-room triplex and its rooftop park had appeared in several magazines, and it had been featured on *Lifestyles of the Rich and Famous*—in no way undermined my enjoyment of the visual and aural assault that followed: the twenty-nine-foot-high living room with its erupting fountain and vaulted ceiling decorated with neo-Romantic frescoes; the two-story dining room with its carved ivory frieze ("I admit that the ivory's kind of a no-no"); the onyx columns with marble capitals that had come from "a castle in Italy"; the chandelier that originally hung in "a castle in Austria"; the African blue-onyx lavatory. As we admired the view of Central Park, to the north, he said, "This is the greatest apartment ever built. There's never been anything like it. There's no apartment like this anywhere. It was harder to build this apartment than the rest of the building. A lot of it I did just to see if it could be done. All the very wealthy people who think they know great apartments come here and they say, 'Donald, forget it. This is the greatest.'" Very few touches suggested that real people actually lived there—where was it, exactly, that Trump sat around in his boxers, eating roast-beef sandwiches, channel surfing, and scratching where it itched? Where was it that Marla threw her jogging clothes?—but no matter. "Come here, I'll show you how life works," he said, and we turned a couple of corners and wound up in a sitting room that had a Renoir* on one wall and a view that extended beyond the Statue of Liberty. "My apartments that face the Park go for twice as much as the apartments that face south. But I consider *this* view to be more beautiful than *that* view, especially at night. As a cityscape, it can't be beat."

* Years later, I became aware that the picture, *La Loge*, was a Renoir only if a reproduction of a Renoir qualifies as a Renoir. The original hangs in the Courtauld Institute of Art in London.

We then drove down to 40 Wall Street, where members of a German television crew were waiting for Trump to show them around. ("This will be the finest office building anywhere in New York. Not just downtown—anywhere in New York.") Along the way, we stopped for a light at Forty-second Street and First Avenue. The driver of a panel truck in the next lane began waving, then rolled down his window and burbled, "I never see you in person!" He was fortyish, wore a blue watch cap, and spoke with a Hispanic inflection. "But I see you a lot on TV."

"Good," said Trump. "Thank you. I think."

"Where's Marla?"

"She's in Louisiana, getting ready to host the Miss U.S.A. pageant. You better watch it. O.K.?"

"O.K., I promise," said the man in the truck. "Have a nice day, Mr. Trump. And have a *profitable* day."

"Always."

Later, Trump said to me, "You want to know what total recognition is? I'll tell you how you know you've got it. When the Nigerians on the street corners who don't speak a word of English, who have no clue, who're selling watches for some guy in New Jersey—

82

when you walk by and those guys say, 'Trump! Trump!' that's total recognition."

Next, we headed north, to Mount Kisco, in Westchester County—specifically to Seven Springs, a fifty-five-room limestone-and-granite Georgian splendor completed in 1917 by Eugene Meyer, the father of Katharine Graham. If things proceeded according to plan, within a year and a half the house would become the centerpiece of the Trump Mansion at Seven Springs, a golf club where anyone willing to part with two hundred and fifty thousand dollars could tee up. As we approached, Trump made certain I paid attention to the walls lining the driveway. "Look at the quality of this granite. Because I'm like, you know, into quality. Look at the quality of that wall. Hand-carved granite, and the same with the house." Entering a room where two men were replastering a ceiling, Trump exulted, "We've got the pros here! You don't see too many plasterers anymore. I take a union plasterer from New York and bring him up here. You know why? Because he's the best." We canvassed the upper floors and then the basement, where Trump sized up the bowling alley as a potential spa. "This is very much Mar-a-Lago all over again," he said. "A great building, great land, great location. Then the question is what to do with it."

From the rear terrace, Trump mapped out some holes of the golf course: an elevated tee above a par three, across a ravine filled with laurel and dogwood; a couple of parallel par fours above the slope that led to a reservoir. Then he turned to me and said, "I bought this whole thing for seven and a half million dollars. People ask, 'How'd you do that?' I said, 'I don't know.' Does that make sense?" Not really, nor did his next utterance: "You know, nobody's ever seen a granite house before."

Granite? Nobody? Never? In the history of humankind? Impressive.

A few months ago, Marla Maples Trump, with a straight face, told an interviewer about life with hubby: "He really has the desire to have me be more of the traditional wife. He definitely wants his dinner promptly served at seven. And if he's home at six-thirty it should be ready by six-thirty." Oh well, so much for that.

In Trump's office the other morning, I asked whether, in light of his domestic shuffle, he planned to change his living arrangements. He smiled for the first time that day and said, "Where am I going to live? That might be the most difficult question you've asked so far. I want to finish the work on my apartment at Trump International. That should take a few months, maybe two, maybe six. And then I think I'll live there for maybe six months. Let's just say, for a period of time. The buildings always work better when I'm living there."

What about the Trump Tower apartment? Would that sit empty?

"Well, I wouldn't sell that. And, of course, there's no one who would ever build an apartment like that. The penthouse at Trump International isn't nearly as big. It's maybe seven thousand square feet. But it's got a living room that is the most spectacular residential room in New York. A twenty-five-foot ceiling. I'm telling you, the best room anywhere. Do you understand?"

I think I did: the only apartment with a better view than the best apartment in the world was the same apartment. Except for the one across the Park, which had the most spectacular living room in the world. No one had ever seen a granite house before. And, most important, every square inch belonged to Trump, who had aspired to and achieved the ultimate luxury, an existence unmolested by the rumbling of a soul. "Trump"—a fellow with universal recognition but with a suspicion that an interior life was an intolerable inconvenience, a creature everywhere and nowhere, uniquely capable of inhabiting it all at once, all alone.

BELIEVE ME

I used to think the funniest thing I'd ever heard Donald Trump say was when, one day in his office, he handed me a two-page unaudited personal financial statement and said, "I've never shown this to a reporter before." I knew this could not possibly be true, just as I knew that his alleged net worth ($2.25 billion) was fictitious. He could have equally credibly assured me that he'd negotiated an option to buy Canada. The only thing that might have amused me more would have been if he'd offered me the certified scorecards from when he played golf alone.

Then, as now, I never cared how much Trump said he was "worth." I remain confident that a true appraisal would be a fraction of whatever figure he claims on a given day. His main selling point as a presidential candidate, of course, is that he's a super-genius incredibly successful dealmaker who will make fabulous fantastic deals that will have every citizen's head spinning—a refreshing contrast to the serially "disastrous" deals of his Oval Office predecessors. "I'm *really* rich," Trump likes to say. Or the long form: "Part of the beauty of me is that I am very rich." (As ever, in the eye of the beholder.)

In the early nineties, Trump stiffed his creditors for eight-hundred million dollars, give or take. Later, whenever this fact was mentioned, he reflexively insisted that it had never happened. Except that it had, and subsequently no one with a lick of sense was willing to lend him fresh money. Gail Collins, of *The New York Times*, once referred to him as a "financially embattled thousandaire." Trump sent her a copy of one of her columns with, across her photograph, the chivalrous scrawl "The Face of a Dog!" In 2005, Timothy O'Brien, then a *Times* colleague of Collins, published a book, *TrumpNation: The Art of Being The Donald*, in which he estimated Trump's net worth at $150 million to $250 million. Not unpredictably, Trump sued for $5 billion, alleging that this lowball calculation constituted libel and defamation. The case was dismissed four years later, after Trump acknowledged during a deposition: "My net worth fluctuates, and it goes up and down with markets and with attitudes and with feelings, even my own feelings . . . and that can change rapidly from day to day."

Given that O'Brien later stated, "My lawyers stripped the bark off of him," I admit it's awfully Trumpish of me to claim credit for his salutary outcome. Nevertheless I must mention that, early in the proceedings, I wrote a short piece in *The New Yorker* advising O'Brien to string Trump along rather than immediately cutting him a ten-figure check. I confessed my envy and, in an open letter of sorts to Trump, begged him to try to make my life miserable, too: "Please, Donald . . . Once and for all, sue me. I need the aggravation. Not to mention the royalties." For a change, I didn't hear back. I'm guessing his subscription had expired.

The sage observation that "I wouldn't believe Donald Trump if his tongue were notarized"—courtesy of Alair Townsend, a former deputy mayor of New York City—offered a simple enough rule to live by, and it's never gone out of fashion. A healthy democracy depends, I suppose, upon the vigilance of a free press whose members feel personally affronted by the brazen mendacity of the powerful. I'm just not that touchy. With Trump, I always knew that it wasn't my intelligence per se that was being insulted by the transparent distortions that burbled from his lips; that was just the way the man talked. I feel confident that Trump never budged from his initial estimation of me as a hapless schmuck. Still, given his campaign-trail pronouncements about the press—"scum . . . terrible . . . lying disgusting people . . . I hate some of these people, I hate 'em"—I'd say we got along swell. As long as he kept talking, what could go wrong? Unless Trump was having an off day megalomania-wise, he was never not good copy. Before he lifted his eyes to the horizon and decided the moment was ripe to take over the entire world, the hometown press dreaded the prospect that he might freeze us out. How would we feed our families?

. . .

The ascendant Trump familiar to New Yorkers during the '70s, '80s, and '90s was hardly harmless. He possessed a talent for inducing targeted outrage—the hair-trigger litigiousness helped—among public officials, real-estate competitors, business partners, casino shareholders and bondholders, and tenants in buildings that bore his name. He called Ed Koch, a three-term mayor, a "moron." He said, "The city under Ed Koch is a disaster." (Sound familiar?) Koch returned the favor with "greedy, greedy, greedy"—if Trump was "squealing like a stuck pig, I must have done something right." Still, the damage in those days was relatively localized. Whatever games Trump was playing, the spoils in retrospect seem quaintly small-potatoes.

In 1975, when Trump was pursuing his first major Manhattan real-estate venture, the Grand Hyatt New York, on the site of the old Commodore Hotel, the then-mayor, Abe Beame, was a Brooklyn Democratic-machine-bred career civil servant—i.e., a malleable hack—susceptible to the blandishments of Trump's Brooklyn-clubhouse-wired father and loan guarantor. Donald the dauphin presumed the license to write his own rules, and it worked. He squeezed unprecedented tax abatements from a functionally bankrupt municipal government. The monster rose from the laboratory table and walked.

During the demolition to clear the Fifth Avenue site for Trump Tower, five years later, he approved the destruction of a pair of massive limestone art-deco bas-relief panels above the entrance to the erstwhile Bonwit Teller department store. Trump had promised to donate the panels to the Metropolitan Museum of Art but later decided that properly removing them was too expensive and time-consuming. He wanted his building built. Shrewdly, he had covered his ass with a made-to-order fall guy—an in-over-his-head demolition contractor who, as it happened, employed a wrecking crew of grossly underpaid, mistreated, distinctly undocumented Polish laborers. (So much for securing the borders.)

Wollman Rink, a public ice rink in Central Park, had closed for repairs that same year. Six years and more than twelve million dollars later, it still hadn't reopened. Trump Tower's first tenants had long since settled in. Thus was launched Trump's first great public-relations coup: completing the rink renovation in three and a half months, for two million two hundred fifty thousand dollars. The following year, at the invitation of a Republican activist in southern New Hampshire, he emerged from a sporty black helicopter to deliver a Rotary Club speech. Among the locals who greeted him, some held signs that said TRUMP IN '88 and VOTE FOR AN EN-TRUMP-ENEUR. A few months later, after a television appearance, he received a Dear Donald note from Richard Nixon: "I did not see the program, but Mrs. Nixon told me that you were great ... As you can imagine, she is an expert on politics and she predicts that whenever you decide to run for office you will be a winner!"

Thanks, Dick.

Next came a Kabuki theater press tour of the underbelly of the temporarily out-of-commission Williamsburg Bridge. Trump had enlisted a senior transportation official in the Reagan administration as a prop, under the pretext that Trump was just the fellow to overhaul the entire city's crumbling infrastructure.

Because bankruptcy tribulations and domestic disarray soon got in the way, 1988 would be the last presidential year for a while in which he would contrive a Trump for Emperor charade. He was back at it in 2000 and 2004, and in 2012 he performed an especially ostentatious Prince of Denmark routine before bowing out. That he possessed no core beliefs, no describable political philosophy, and not an iota of curiosity about the practicalities of policy and governance was irrelevant—to Trump, anyway—and seemed not to factor in the decision. He had been variously a Democrat, a Republican, an Independent, and a possible candidate for the Reform Party. His intrinsic loyalty? In business, politics, and life he had remained faithful to only one constituent. And a single theme: *Trump. Me. Look.*

Until June 16, 2015, when he descended the escalator in the Trump Tower atrium and, with paid actors wearing MAKE AMERICA GREAT AGAIN! T-shirts cheering him on, inaugurated his courageous effort to make *Mexican* synonymous with *rapist* and *drug smuggler*, I never thought he'd take the leap.

• • •

Sensible individuals of sterling repute—Jon Stewart, Stephen Colbert, Bill Maher—judged Trump's campaign launch an occasion for celebration. Not a particularly patriotic verdict, but who could blame them. The world's richest lode of potential satire had just been discovered! For once, I demurred. I have never disapproved of the public ridicule of self-important blowhards. This time, though, I wasn't in the mood. Only rarely during the Obama era had Trump's antics yielded satisfying retribution. What appeared to be good for late-night comedy I felt would not be good for the Democrats. (Certainly not for Republicans.) It could not be good for America.* It boded ill for humanity.

Otherwise I misread the moment, along with one hundred percent of the commentariat. We *knew* that Trump would be gone long before the primaries. We got it completely wrong. Before grasping just how mistaken I was about his prospects, I vowed not to jump in. Why write about this extended exhibition of Trumpian autoeroticism when everyone else already was? No need to feed the beast. Better it should starve of neglect.

Over the weeks and months that followed, as

---

* Leslie Moonves, the president and CEO of CBS, let the truth out a while back: "It may not be good for America, but it's damn good for CBS. . . . This is going to be a very good year for us. Sorry. It's a terrible thing to say. But, bring it on, Donald. Keep going." I keep this unabashed confession in mind whenever I go channel-surfing, lest I be tempted to alight on CBS.

Trump spewed taunts, insults, threats, and dog-whistle-free bigotry—expanding his repertoire from Mexicans to the planet's 1.6 billion Muslims—his poll numbers vindicated his methods. Thousands of real voters with real fears and long festering grievances thronged to his rallies. Among them were manifestly unrepentant haters, but that was not the majority sentiment. These were citizens whose resentment and anger had steeped in the blatant chronic bad faith of their elected representatives. For the time being, Trump would overcome his germophobic dread of waving fields of outstretched paws. With his genius for counterfeit fellow-feeling, he knew exactly which buttons to push and when. (During a midwinter meeting with the editorial board of the *Times*, he slipped up and gave the game away: "You know, if it gets a little boring, if I see people starting to sort of, maybe thinking about leaving, I can sort of tell the audience, I just say, 'We will build the wall!'—and they go nuts."* Indeed they did.) Trump loomed as an as-

---

* Trump's admirers were not the only ones going nuts. One note-worthy dissenter was the former El Presidente de Mexico Vicente Fox: "I'm not going to pay for that fucking wall!"

pirational figure, a pseudo-populist self-proclaimed multi-billionaire whose contempt for the customary protocols of the reviled Washington establishment bound him to his adherents in a mutual intoxication. A cocktail of bogus facts, stirred by fear, naïveté, and an indifference to pragmatic exigencies. A zeal only loosely tethered to reality. "I love the poorly educated!" he crowed. They loved him back.

That he did not sound or behave like a typical politician won him points for authenticity. No one in the congregation seemed to mind—or even register— that an authentic corporeal Donald Trump did not exist. There was only *Trump*—in the flesh, as it were, a bloated bloviator in a navy suit and bright primary-colored necktie, with a laboriously tended pumpkin-pink coif that grew nowhere in nature. All was artifice. He greeted each assembly with a profession of love, congratulating the crowd for being three times larger than it in fact was. At each subsequent whistle-stop it grew larger yet. Trump held forth with bladder-testing stamina. But what was that coming out of his mouth? A stump speech of rambling self-aggrandizement and tough-talk sound bites: bigness, greatness, getting screwed, getting even, China,

Mexico, Japan, the system's rigged, losing, winning, head-spinning, an endless infomercial about his putative riches and fantastic fabulousness—flowing in intermittently filtered free association.

The bombast spoke plainly of his tactics, if not necessarily of his objectives. I doubted that winning the Republican nomination, let alone winning the general election, could be Trump's genuine desire. The most logical rationale for his candidacy was the abiding obsession with his ever-metastasizing brand. From the podium he peddled Trump water, Trump wine, and Trump Steaks (an obsolete product). He spoke of himself in the third person: "Nobody would be tougher on ISIS than Donald Trump"; "Missouri just confirmed a victory for Donald Trump"; "Rand Paul is doing so badly he figures he has to go out and attack Trump." When a protester who repeatedly shouted "Not all Mexicans are rapists, not all Muslims are terrorists!" received a police escort to the exit, Trump said, "He looks like an Elvis impersonator. That's strange because the Elvis impersonators loved Donald Trump." He claimed that "on women's issues and health issues there will be nobody better than Donald Trump." This last load of chutzpah from the itchy-Twitter-(short)-fingered author of: "If Hillary Clinton can't satisfy her husband what makes her think she can satisfy America?"

Here was an ostensible aspiring leader of the free world whose transparent anxieties about the adequacy of his genitalia dominated more than one news cycle. Watching the televised debate the first time Trump *went there*, I laughed, then winced. Nineteen years earlier, recounting the unraveling of his first marriage, his adultery with his future-second-ex-wife Marla Maples, and its attendant *New York Post* headline BEST SEX I'VE EVER HAD, I wrote that "an acquaintance of Marla's blabbed about Donald's swordsmanship." Or so the *Post* had reported, but *what had I been thinking?* Yikes. No such thing had happened. The only plausible blabber was Donald himself. *Plus ça change.*

The other pretenders to the Republican nomination, mostly a woefully ineffectual bunch, were reduced to alternating incredulity and strangulated dudgeon. I sympathized. Sort of. Much of the Fourth Estate, meanwhile, first by not taking Trump seriously, and then by *taking* him seriously, assumed roles as his witless enablers. For months, Trump played them like suckers at a sideshow. The more airtime and ink they gave him, the more he vilified them. No matter how much invective he showered, goading the rabble to hurl abuse at the unfortunate hostages in the media enclosure, the cameras kept running. At moments, the spectacle was disturbing to the point of unwatchability. On the distant sideline (specifically, my living room sofa), my shaming secret was that I couldn't look away.

• • •

The novelty of the Trump campaign extended to its slogan, "Make America Great Again!" This was a direct lift from Ronald Reagan's 1980 "Let's Make America Great Again," but Trump brandished it with an unambiguous nativist bite. In no time, the decoders rendered it "Make America White Again!," a formulation suggesting that Trump's anti-Muslim immigration absolutism, for instance, expressed a yearning for an ethnically cleansed U.S.A.—manifest destiny by other means. I don't see it that way. Trump-branded buildings, long regarded as safe havens for foreign flight capital, have always been popular with super-luxury-inclined multinational non-Caucasian plutocrats. (Among them, no doubt, a fair representation of Third World kleptocrats.)

As Trump drew closer to clinching the nomination, his recently hired political strategist, Paul Manafort, embarked upon an improbable effort to make him appear more presidential. Or, failing that, perhaps less Donald-like. Using the Mayflower Hotel, in Washington, as window dressing, he delivered what was billed as a major foreign policy address, reading from a prepared text for only the second time in his campaign. Its isolationist overtones ("'America first' will be the overriding theme of my administration") didn't square with his penchant for off-the-cuff warmongering: "You know the thing I'll be great at that people aren't thinking? And I do very well at it. Military. I am the toughest guy. I will rebuild our military. It will be so strong, and so powerful, and so great."

Challenged by Chris Matthews to assure "the whole world" that he would never consider using nuclear weapons *in Europe*, Trump replied, "I—I'm not going to take it off the table."

His strategy for defeating ISIS? "I would bomb the shit out of them. I would just bomb those suckers."

Because Trump was Trump, little was made of his history of dodging the draft. A high number in the

1969 draft lottery would have helped him avoid military service if he hadn't already obtained a medical deferment for heel spurs. Asked by a reporter in Iowa which heel had been afflicted, he drew a blank, then said, "You'll have to look it up."

As it was, Trump felt that he had already served his country nobly. During his high school years at New York Military Academy, he said, "I always thought I was in the military."

Did he mean the same military as Senator John McCain—the former U.S. Navy aviator shot down and severely injured during a Vietnam War mission in 1967, followed by six years as a North Vietnamese prisoner-of-war, during two of which he was repeatedly beaten and tortured? The same McCain who Trump had disparaged as "not a war hero"?*

It was unmistakably the same fearless and valiant Trump, who once, while discussing with Howard Stern the risks of sexually transmitted diseases, had observed, "It's amazing. I've been so lucky in terms

---

* This bouquet is unlikely to endure as Trump's most judicious ad lib. Having inserted his foot in his mouth, he kept chewing until he was up to his kneecap. "He's not a war hero. He's a war hero because he was captured. I like people that weren't captured."

of that whole world. It is a dangerous world out there. It's scary. It's like Vietnam. It is my personal Vietnam. I feel like a great and very brave soldier."*

. . .

Another reliable Trump trope, usually punctuated by a quick headshake, was *believe me*: "I would build a great wall—and nobody builds walls better than me, believe me . . . I would have Mexico pay for it. Believe me, they will pay for it. . . . I didn't come here tonight to pander to you about Israel. That's what politicians do: all talk, no action, believe me . . . I've devoted so much time over my life to Israel, and the other politicians, they can talk but, believe me, they haven't done what I've done."

This would be easy to gloss over as a trivial rhetorical tic if the speaker had not long since situated himself along a credibility spectrum between *highly dubious* and *are-you-out-of-your-mind?* Each iteration of *believe me* begged the question at the heart of the

---

* Trump also concurred with Stern's insight that "every vagina is like a potential land mine."

Trumpian enigma: did he believe himself? In *The Art of the Deal*, his first best-selling paean to Donald J. Trump, he boasted about his predilection for "truthful hyperbole . . . an innocent form of exaggeration—and a very effective form of promotion." *Truthful hyperbole*, à la Trump, is not mere oxymoron. Politely put, it's total horseshit. What started out as a marketing maxim to justify Trump's carefree dissembling he would eventually leverage into a new variation of the American dream: an artfully fabricated, hermetic, alternate reality.

The night that Trump carried 53 percent of the vote in Indiana and was declared by the chair of the National Republican Committee to be "the presumtive [sic] GOP nominee," Ted Cruz packed up his reptilian charisma and returned to Texas to begin plotting his resurrection four years hence. As he departed, Trump praised him as "one hell of a competitor . . . a tough, smart guy." Trump's real going-away gift, though, had been delivered that very morning, when he parroted a *National Enquirer* story suggesting that Cruz's father had been complicit with Lee Harvey Oswald in the assassination of John F. Kennedy.

By then, Trump had a demonstrated propensity for

exploiting epochal national tragedies to suit his purposes. He relished describing having watched "thousands and thousands of people" cheering in Jersey City, New Jersey—directly across the Hudson River from the World Trade Center—as the twin towers collapsed on 9/11. Jersey City is home to a substantial Arab population. Several news organizations investigated and found zero evidence to support Trump's fantasy. Politifact.com, the nonpartisan fact-checking project of the *Tampa Bay Times*, designated the Jersey City whopper its 2015 "Lie of the Year." When George Stephanopoulos, of ABC News, confronted Trump, pointing out that the story had circulated for some time as an Internet canard, he replied, "It was on television. I saw it." Fact checkers at the *Washington Post* had awarded him four "Pinocchios." Trump persisted. It played quite well in the Deep South.

"Maybe truthful to a fault" was how he humbly described himself to a crowd in North Carolina. After a Trump town hall in Wisconsin that aired on CNN, the *Huffington Post* scrutinized the transcript and counted "71 separate instances in which Trump made a claim that was inaccurate, misleading, or deeply questionable." This occurred within a single hour, commercial breaks included. On a different occasion, in a less punctilious exercise, I kept a tally of my own during CNN's broadcast of a multi-candidate town hall in South Carolina. Trump was in peak form. Along with the usual Obamacare-is-dead and build-the-wall blah-blah, I most enjoyed:

"I'm not a bully. No, I'm not a bully at all."

"I have a great temperament."

"I think I was really, really a good parent because I put my children above everything."

"I'm a smart person."

"We have Caroline Kennedy negotiating car deals and trade deals with . . . Japan."

"I get a lot of publicity. I don't necessarily like it . . . No, it's true . . . You know what, it's true."

. . .

It is deeply unfair to say that Trump lies all the time. I would never suggest that he lies when he's asleep. On the other hand, he famously gets by on only four hours a night. I suspect this might be less a function of requiring very little sleep than of Trump's agitation at being unable to manipulate his unconscious. Four hours might be as much loss of control as he can tolerate. We'll never know, and neither will Trump. He told one biographer, "I don't like to analyze myself because I might not like what I see." This indicates either extraordinary restraint and self-awareness or an utter lack thereof. Or both.

It might also presage a global very bad something. At moments, I reassure myself that Trump doesn't truly wish to be President; he just doesn't want to lose the election. And while it lasts, he wants to savor the sound of his name roared by the multitude after he heaves a chunk of raw sirloin like "Would I approve waterboarding? You bet your ass I would. You bet your ass. In a heartbeat. In a heartbeat. I would approve more than that." Win or lose, I wonder how long it will take Trump's bedrock partisans to grasp that they've been played. Trump was barely out of his Wharton School short pants when the Republican Party devised its Southern strategy—exploiting racial and culture war grievances to persuade disaffected working-class white men to vote contrary to their economic self-interests. He didn't invent the bait-and-switch; he is just its latest, and most enthusiastic, practitioner.

Watching Trump work his base, I'm invariably reminded of the trip we once made to Atlantic City, where he and Vanna White charmed the expectant patrons of the Trump Castle, then the most conspicuously failing of his failing casino properties. Vanna was on hand for a "ceremonial first pull" of a newly installed *Wheel of Fortune*–themed slot machine— there were thirteen of them—whereupon the star-struck pensioners surged forward to part with that week's grocery budget. As we headed for the exit, Trump said to me, "This is what we do. What can I tell you?"

Sometime after Election Day, my plan is to write to Trump and, as is my habit, enclose a gift. Right now I'm thinking maybe a book he's never read before. Alexander Hamilton is bigger than ever—Trump likes big, right?—so *The Federalist Papers* for sure. While I'm at it, also the Constitution. No matter how busy he is, I expect to hear back. Cannot wait to hear back is really more like it.

Donald, please. Don't be such a stranger.

ACKNOWLEDGMENTS

My thanks to:

Colleagues at *The New Yorker* current and former, including Roger Angell, Peter Canby, Cynthia Cotts, Amy Davidson, Bruce Diones, Jeffrey Frank, Ann Goldstein, Mary Norris, Brenda Phipps, David Remnick, Dorothy Wickenden, and Daniel Zalewski.

Tina Brown, for the gift that has kept giving.

For research assistance, Reid Singer (who is like a son to me). Also, Jake Lahut.

At Crown, Tim Duggan and Will Wolfslau.

Ian Frazier, Melissa Harris, John McPhee, Jeffrey Posternak, Jeb Singer, Betsy Singer, Timothy Singer, Paul Mailhot-Singer—each of you knows why.

The many journalists who across the years have assiduously reported about Donald Trump, in the process potentially putting themselves in harm's way, especially Michael D'Antonio, David Cay Johnston, Timothy O'Brien, and the great Wayne Barrett.